THE
SCORPIO
ORACLE

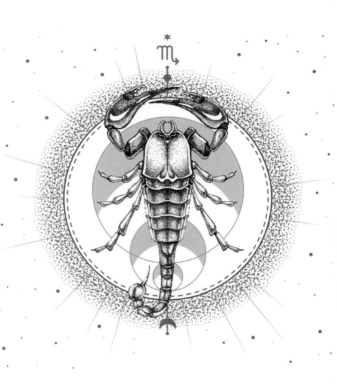

THE SCORPIO ORACLE

INSTANT ANSWERS FROM YOUR COSMIC SELF

STELLA FONTAINE

greenfinch

Introduction

Welcome to your zodiac oracle,
carefully crafted especially for you
Scorpio, and brimming with the
wisdom of the universe.

**Is there a tricky-to-answer question niggling at you
and you need an answer?**

Whenever you're unsure whether to say 'yes' or 'no',
whether to go back or to carry on, whether to trust
or to turn away, make some time for a personal
session with your very own oracle. Drawing on your
astrological profile, your zodiac oracle will guide
you in understanding, interpreting and answering
those burning questions that life throws your way.
Discovering your true path will become an
enlightening journey of self-actualization.

Humans have long cast their eyes heavenwards to seek answers from the universe. For millennia the sun, moon and stars have been our constant companions as they repeat their paths and patterns across the skies. We continue to turn to the cosmos for guidance, trusting in the deep and abiding wisdom of the universe as we strive for fulfilment, truth and understanding.

The most basic and familiar aspect of astrology draws on the twelve signs of the zodiac, each connected to a unique constellation as well as its own particular colours, numbers and characteristics. These twelve familiar signs are also known as the sun signs: Aries, Taurus, Gemini, Cancer, Leo, Virgo, Libra, Scorpio, Sagittarius, Capricorn, Aquarius and Pisces.

Each sign is associated with an element (fire, air, earth or water), and also carries a particular quality: cardinal (action-takers), fixed (steady and constant) and mutable (changeable and transformational). Beginning to understand these complex combinations, and to recognize the layered influences they bring to bear on your life, will unlock your own potential for personal insight, self-awareness and discovery.

In our data-flooded lives, now more than ever it can be difficult to know where to turn for guidance and advice. With your astrology oracle always by your side, navigating life's twists and turns will become a smoother, more mindful process. Harness the prescience of the stars and tune in to the resonance of your sun sign with this wisdom-packed guide that will lead you to greater self-knowledge and deeper confidence in the decisions you are making. Of course, not all questions are created equal; your unique character, your circumstances and the issues with which you find yourself confronted all add up to a conundrum unlike any other... but with your question in mind and your zodiac oracle in your hand, you're already halfway to the answer.

Scorpio
OCTOBER 23 TO NOVEMBER 21

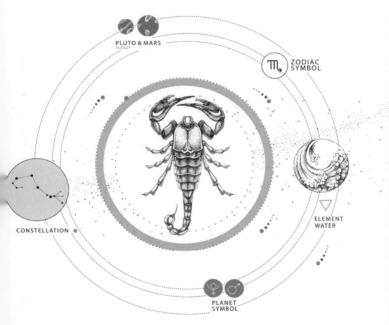

Element: Water
Quality: Fixed
Named for the constellation: Scorpio (the scorpion)
Ruled by: Pluto, Mars
Opposite: Taurus
Characterized by: Courage, passion, resourcefulness
Colour: Reds

How to Use This Book

You can engage with your oracle whenever you
need to but, for best results, create an atmosphere
of calm and quiet, somewhere you will not be
disturbed, making a place for yourself and your
question to take priority. Whether this is a particular
physical area you turn to in times of contemplation,
or whether you need to fence off a dedicated space
within yourself during your busy day, that all
depends on you and your circumstances. Whichever
you choose, it is essential that you actively put other
thoughts and distractions to one side in order to
concentrate upon the question you wish to answer.

Find a comfortable position, cradle this book lightly
in your hands, close your eyes, centre yourself. Focus
on the question you wish to ask. Set your intention
gently and mindfully towards your desire to answer
this question, to the exclusion of all other thoughts
and mind-chatter. Allow all else to float softly away,
as you remain quiet and still, gently watching the
shape and form of the question you wish to address.
Gently deepen and slow your breathing.

Tune in to the ancient resonance of your star sign, the vibrations of your surroundings, the beat of your heart and the flow of life and the universe moving in and around you. You are one with the universe.

Now simply press the book between your palms as you clearly and distinctly ask your question (whether aloud or in your head), then open it at any page. Open your eyes. Your advice will be revealed.

Read it carefully. Take your time turning this wisdom over in your mind, allowing your thoughts to surround it, to absorb it, flow with it, then to linger and settle where they will.

Remember, your oracle will not provide anything as blunt and brutal as a completely literal answer. That is not its role. Rather, you will be gently guided towards the truth you seek through your own consciousness, experience and understanding. And as a result, you will grow, learn and flourish.

Let's begin.

Close your eyes.

Hold the question you want
answered clearly in your mind.

Open your oracle to any page to
reveal your cosmic insight.

Your famous Scorpio
self-assuredness means you are often
certain you know best. But bring some
patience and understanding to
this one; step back to see the
bigger picture.

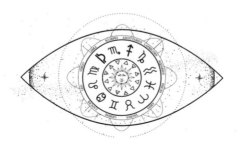

Your indefatigable energy is pushing this question to the front, but are you sure there isn't really another, bigger question you would prefer to answer? Ask again.

Scorpios are top networkers, gifted with an easy knack for understanding the motivations of others. Concern yourself less with how you feel about this issue; try looking at it from someone else's perspective.

When you sense negativity and bad energy, take steps to distance yourself. Do not allow the fixed position of others to limit your options or restrict your ambition – you will only become frustrated.

Strong-willed, enthusiastic,
energetic and staunchly unwavering
once set on a course of action, you
have everything you need already to
hand Scorpio. Step forwards to
meet this one whole-heartedly,
and don't look back or stop
until you are done.

This is an easy one for a
self-sufficient, resourceful Scorpio,
and of course you already know the
answer. You usually do!

Your tirelessly analytical approach means you've been turning this one over in your head for a while now, haven't you? Time for a change.

Scorpios love to rise to a challenge! But along the way, don't forget that vulnerability does not equate to weakness (remember, this applies to you as well as everyone else).

Resist the impulse to clutch
what comes your way tightly in your
pincers; it can only end badly. Hold
only that which serves you
and let the rest of it go.

Trust the depth of your
Scorpio intuition; it is a gift. This
outcome has never been in question;
it is written in the stars.

Success approaches, although
it may turn out to be slightly less
spectacular than you had first hoped.
A stepping-stone path of small wins is
the key to this one, celebrate each
victory along the way.

Different results represent success to different people. In this situation, it may be difficult to understand the outcome, but that's not important for now. It will make more sense later.

Your hard-working tendencies and competitive Scorpio spirit mean you are streets ahead of everyone else when it comes to achieving your goals. But try to ease up on the self-overload; this time, working with others could help make your dreams a reality.

Make the most of Pluto's influence
as your ruling planet, it's time to draw
on those icy reserves of determination.
Hold your nerve and see this through.

Tackle this one head on and with your compass properly aligned Scorpio. Once you have set your course and made a start, don't look back.

Always single-minded Scorpio,
it is worth remembering that
occasionally getting exactly what
you want means a cost to someone
else. You just need to decide whether
you are content to let them pay
the price on your behalf.

Others must manage their own lives, and that means making their own mistakes and learning their own lessons. Much as you may want to help, there is only so much you can do before you are actually damaging their own autonomy Scorpio.

The way you function can
seem cold and calculating to those
who don't understand that you simply
know what you want. But you are a
water sign Scorpio, and keeping it cool
while you formulate your plan is
simply second nature to you.
Do what you do best.

Ruled by Pluto, named for the king of the underworld, you were always going to experience the tension between dark and light more keenly than most. But nothing is forever, everything changes.

Draw on your deep pools of emotional Scorpion energy and resist the urge to turn a blind eye simply because of what it is that you think you want. While half a truth is not really the truth, half a lie is still a lie.

Although you are often mistaken
for a fire sign Scorpio, you are water
through and through. Your depth and
intensity are second to none, and a
powerful intuition flows through
everything you do. The force of your
will can carry others along like a wave
but do pause this time to consider
whether this is really the right
way to behave.

Stress can come for you too
Scorpio, and you need to stop it in
its tracks before it has a chance to
tighten around you and do any serious
damage. Twist out of its grip and
be on your way.

It's not always sunshine or starlight with you; with Pluto bobbing around out there, things can get edgy. Scorpios can be very convincing and there's that legendary sting in the tail to consider, as well. Commit yourself to what matters – build up your own understanding and resources rather than relying on those of others.

Your star sign has gifted you both intuition and imagination, but it is time to bring your legendary willpower into play as well. You will not achieve your full potential without taking a risk.

Having Taurus as your opposite
sign is about to come in pretty handy.
Lower your horns and confront this
challenge head-on; let's find out what
you are capable of.

Your Scorpio curiosity and persistence are well known. Stay true to yourself; others have their own race to run. There is enough of what matters for everyone to take their share.

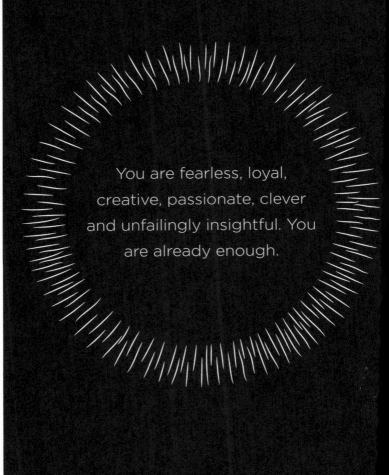

You are fearless, loyal, creative, passionate, clever and unfailingly insightful. You are already enough.

Your strength and passion
are obvious to everyone who meets
you. But don't forget that to truly
allow others to know who you are,
you will have to allow them to see the
real you, the complicated emotional
layers that lie beneath that tough,
protective outer layer.

Leave strategy and process at the door on your way in today; make a decision about the direction you will take and get moving.

Destruction and transformation both come naturally to you, thanks to your ruling planet, Pluto. Within this endless cycle, anything is possible.

As a Scorpio, approaching
any problem with charm, intellect
and complete confidence is second
nature to you. Your talent for flexible
solutions and creative work-arounds
will help you again this time.

Scorpios are naturally secretive;
but this might be a good opportunity
to work on developing trust and
being more open.

Spread the joy by exploring
your own creativity a little more.

Your motivations needn't always
be completely selfless Scorpio, as
long as your actions are pure
and without malice.

If you can manage to resist your usual impulses, someone you normally try to avoid, or perhaps often dismiss, might make you think. Their perspective will help you see this situation in a new light. Keep an open mind.

Your head and heart will both
be required here; resist the urge to
pick a path until you are sure you have
harnessed thought and emotion in
equal measure. Maintain balance
above all else.

Not all obstacles require domination or attack. Perhaps you might simply slink around this one and carry on with what you were doing.

Curb your Scorpio tendencies towards less healthy obsessions, and instead pour your energies into creative outlets and hobbies. You may even discover a talent you didn't know you had.

With Mars on your side as your co-ruling planet, motivation and determination come easily to you... just as long as your heart is committed to your goal. Does what you are aiming for really resonate with you?

No one would ever make the mistake of assuming you are a pushover Scorpio, but that might not stop others trying to take advantage of you now and again. Clearly you don't need telling, but don't bend further than you are comfortable and hold your ground.

Endeavour to remain open to the possibilities that lie ahead. Change is on your horizon, but there is nothing you can do to plan for it. Be ready.

Your reputation is richly deserved Scorpio. But protecting it should not be at the cost of your happiness. Follow your heart and the rest will fall into place.

Casual isn't really the way you play, is it Scorpio? Everything you do, you do with purpose and dedication, and that's completely admirable. It's just that it can also be, well, exhausting. Try to take things a bit easier right now, for yourself and others. Find time for a little peacefulness and a few moments of reflection.

Turning on that Scorpio charm
has been known to convert even the
firmest doubters – you certainly
have a skill for making friends and
maintaining a connections-web that
stretches far and wide. Make the most
of this resource right now, whether
you are looking for information,
for possibilities or for a way to
reposition yourself effectively.

Now is not the time for spontaneity; there is likely only one best outcome. Proceed with caution.

Feeling uncertain and reluctant to engage carries a deeper message that you must pay attention to Scorpio. If your heart and your emotions are in need of some TLC, give them the time and attention they need to rest and repair.

Strive for calm Scorpio, hold yourself back a little and conserve your energy and resources. Whether that means being less forthcoming than usual in terms of sharing your opinions, deciding not to spend money, or resisting the urge to send lots of energy out in various directions, it will be beneficial.

You may have been feeling a little scrambled of late Scorpio; this doesn't happen to you very often, so when it does it can take you by surprise. Your intuition is usually pitch perfect, but you may have been wondering whether it's quite as finely tuned as it used to be. Hold on to your confidence and believe in yourself; this will pass.

Release your control-clasp; a
vice-like grip will make a mess of this
one. Anyway, it is time to have faith in
your star-path. You do not need to
have all the answers in your own mind.
Your direction ahead is already
illuminated.

Go with the peaceful and compassionate option this time – it makes things easier for everyone.

Time to lighten your own load Scorpio; you can't possibly do it all by yourself. Not well, anyway. Simply asking for some support and assistance will bring several willing assistants running – you've helped plenty of people in your time and they'd love the chance to repay the favour.

Sometimes the truth can seem to be such a slippery and subjective beast, it's difficult to know where it might be hiding. Perhaps the best approach is to step back and look at this in a different light Scorpio. Rather than needing to decide where the rights and wrongs lie, it is better just to keep things moving.

All that passion and spark means that you are often mistaken for a fire sign Scorpio, but it's water all the way for you. And, of course, that makes sense, because water wins over fire, every time.

Patience and persistence will be key this time, and for you Scorpio, one of these things is more difficult than the other. Hold your nerve. Bide your time.

Be sure that all those amazing people who are always helping you out know how much you appreciate them. Your habit is to move on quickly, but don't forget those who gave you a hand up.

It is vital that you do what you know to be the right thing. Your value system might not quite balance with everyone else's, but they don't have to live your life. Run your own race.

Resist the temptation to add
a bit more fire to this one, then store
it in your 'dramas' box; just watch and
wait. It will resolve itself without
your intervention.

Your enthusiasm and positivity may well have a major impact on others at the moment Scorpio, and this will reflect back on you in turn. Spreading the love is all upside.

You take a lot of inspiration
from Taurus, your opposite sign,
and you have no problem pulling a
bit of determination out of the bag.
Combined with your dynamic drive
and distinct competitive instinct,
it makes you the very definition of a
force to be reckoned with – your
opponents should simply take a seat.

Simplify your approach by building up a more comprehensive base-layer of understanding. Your commitment to the best outcome will ensure you fix your focus on the task at hand. Others will appreciate it.

Although it might pain you to admit it Scorpio, you do not always have all the answers. In a time of uncertainty, or just plain not-knowing, have the foresight to quickly own up to this gap in your knowledge.

Be careful not to let drive tip over into dominance Scorpio: it can be a fine line, and that famous sting in your tail makes you a deadly opponent. Ask yourself whether it's really worth it.

For the greatest chance at contentment, channel that incredible Scorpio intensity into connecting and closeness.

You may not necessarily
see yourself as creative Scorpio,
but creativity presents in many
different forms. Your second-to-none
problem-solving, and gift for
recognizing and crafting beautiful
patterns and sequences, definitely
qualify you to join the creativity crowd.

The energy of those you love will
be with you every step of the way as
you face this next stage of challenges.
Whether you see them or not, know
that they are alongside you.
You are not alone.

You have an insatiable fascination
with both endings and beginnings
Scorpio, it's the fluff in the middle that
holds less appeal for you. Your talent
for getting straight to the point is
well-known; use it now.

Intuition is a powerful force
for any Scorpio, and you have a
seemingly effortless gift for
understanding others and getting
quickly to the heart of what makes
them tick. Go with what you know.

Others are drawn to your heart and humour; your imagination, intuition and creativity guarantee that plenty of people will always seek the pleasure of your company. You need only accept the best of them. Be selective.

Yes, you can. But that doesn't
mean you should. Be careful Scorpio,
and examine your reasons closely
before making a move or sharpening
up that sting to a fine point.

All that careful planning and
hard work will pay off Scorpio –
positives and rewards will find their
way to your door. Just be sure you
allow yourself the time and headspace
to truly relish them. You deserve it.

Dedicated and diligent as you
are Scorpio, it is essential that you
find balance with some excitement
and build in time for letting go.
Tunnel-vision will blind you to many of
the opportunities the waves are
washing up at your feet.

Sinking under the surface and
ignoring the world outside for a while
is an important Scorpio recharging
skill. Although you might worry about
losing control, that is extremely
unlikely to happen. And the big plus
is that you will soon be back
up and running.

Scorpio loves to conquer, while your opposite, Taurus, prefers to connect and maintain a peaceful approach. In these opposites there is a balance, an equilibrium brought about by the push and pull. Make your decision with this in mind.

'Want' can be a battleground
for you Scorpio, light and dark,
passion and friction all tangled up in
that big messy ball. It doesn't all have
to go this way though; you can make a
conscious decision to approach
this differently.

With your star sign ruled by both Pluto (king of the underworld) and Mars (god of war), and the bull-headed Taurus as your opposite, your journey was never going to be a gentle, rose-strewn ramble across a sunny lawn, and yet here you are. Well done! Now onwards.

This is the time to draw on
that magnetic personality of yours
and find the best way to ask the right
question. It will all be easy from there.
The answer will reveal itself, right in
front of you. Then all you have to
do is go with it.

Confronted with others' opinions
you might want to bite back and
perhaps wave a cautionary sting in the
air. Instead of adopting a potentially
confrontational stance, first look for a
route around the problem; it will be
much more efficient and expend
far less energy. Win, win.

Build in a break so your strategic brain can rest today... always planning your next move will mean you risk missing the moments that make the now. Focus on feelings and the familiar; allow your deeper Scorpion intuition to guide your moves.

If you find yourself unable to concentrate right now, go with it. Perhaps your subconscious is distracting you from the task at hand in order to draw your attention to something you might not otherwise notice...

Resist your Scorpio urge to push,
control and manipulate this into the
shape you want it to take. If you spend
all your time trying to make it into
something it's not, you may miss the
most important details.

'Ambitious' and 'reward-loving' are two Scorpion traits that complement each other particularly well. Putting in the time and effort virtually guarantees that you will reap the kinds of rewards you particularly value.

You are what you do, not what you say. Empty words and hollow promises don't sit well with you, whether you are on the giving end or the receiving end of them. Don't be tempted to sidestep your own ethics – your integrity has carried you this far and served you well.

Bluntness and candour don't always find a warm welcome Scorpio; even when you think you know your audience well. Watch your words and rein in the sarcasm; sharp words will not land gently or without injury.

Time to ease up on trying to run every show Scorpio. You don't need top billing for every circus that comes to town; take a night off and sit in the audience now and then. Give others their chance to shine; it will reflect well on you.

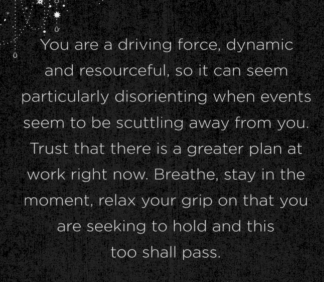

You are a driving force, dynamic and resourceful, so it can seem particularly disorienting when events seem to be scuttling away from you. Trust that there is a greater plan at work right now. Breathe, stay in the moment, relax your grip on that you are seeking to hold and this too shall pass.

You know that there is a better way to go about this, despite the fact it may seem a little more difficult at this point. A fresh approach is required Scorpio. Don't become disheartened though.

Increasing spontaneity is a good move for you Scorpio; especially given your usual impulse to adopt a planned and strategic approach to pretty much everything you do. Others may feel differently about it, but you will have to leave their feelings with them to untangle – it's not something you can help them with.

Scorpio is a water sign, at risk
of absorbing toxic energies but quick
to clear and clean if you maintain a
conscious focus. Your natural touch
serves you well. Maintain
your energy flow.

Of course, anything is possible, especially for you Scorpio. But you might need to take a paddle around this one, to view it from new angles. The direction of approach will make the difference to your chances of success.

You will very likely need some
help now Scorpio. Luckily, you are
surrounded by adoring supporters, so
make the most of them. And don't
forget to say 'thank you' afterwards.

Throw that famous Scorpio intuition into high gear, then sit back and enjoy the ride. Possibility is more complex and infinitely more beautiful than just what you can see on the surface.

Slip into the water while you think
this one through Scorpio... take a bath
or shower, go for a swim or even a
walk in the rain. It's important to keep
refreshing your thoughts, to
avoid becoming stuck.

Jealousy and judgement haunt Scorpios particularly hard, and while they are difficult guests to accommodate, occasionally they deliver valuable wisdom from your subconscious. Is there a responsibility or a commitment you have been neglecting? A promise broken? Have you kept your end of the bargain? Try to figure out what's really going on.

Possessiveness easily leads into paranoia, if you allow it room to grow. Snuff this one out as quickly as you can – it is a negative energy-sap that will distort your view and alter your perception. Keep to the light side Scorpio.

Even though Scorpios are not ones to forget, you will need to forgive the mistakes that have been made, whether by you or by someone else. Don't let go of the wisdom you have gained but know that moving on is the only practical solution here.

Both outgoing and reserved,
adaptable, quick-to-laugh and
frequently led by your intuition, you've
got everything going for you. Add to
this your talents for deep thinking and
mental agility, and remember you
almost always find a way.
Trust yourself.

Your instinct is strong.
Think less and act more.

Keep that self-critical streak in check Scorpio; your own harsh thoughts can damage you just as surely as sharp words hurt others.

Maintaining the momentum of recent changes will be a positive move for you Scorpio – keep it rolling. Unpredictability can bring some powerful opportunities when you hold yourself open to all possibilities.

Switch off the screens and embrace some downtime today; you will only keep bringing your best game if you allow your energy to replenish. You'll be ready to face the world (and those unavoidable challenges) again in no time.

Your intelligent and measured approach rarely fails you Scorpio; don't be tempted to do this someone else's way, for whatever reason. The decision to aim for a system-shaking change is rarely made well as a knee-jerk reaction. Sleep on it.

You know through experience that
the undecorated truth is not always
well received. Counsel others to
suspend their judgement and, if they
must have their say, to consider
all likely outcomes first.

Rather than wading straight in, adopt an observer role in some of the more fiery conversations that are taking place at the moment Scorpio. Gather your information carefully and keep an eye out for patterns, facts and inconsistencies. When the time comes for your voice to be heard, you will be significantly better informed.

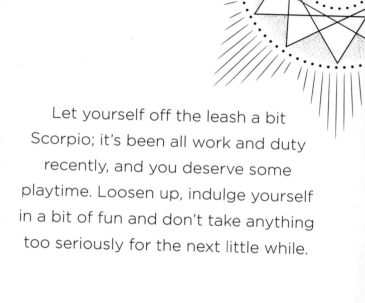

Let yourself off the leash a bit
Scorpio; it's been all work and duty
recently, and you deserve some
playtime. Loosen up, indulge yourself
in a bit of fun and don't take anything
too seriously for the next little while.

Impatient as you may be to sort this one out Scorpio, be mindful of the situation you find yourself in and resist the urge to charge blindly ahead without sufficient preparation. Be sure you are certain of the facts and details before you proceed.

Set aside your Scorpion strategizing and harness your confidence and courage instead; there is some plain-speaking to be done now. You need to clear up any confusion or misunderstanding that has arisen, whether from something as simple as different approaches or perhaps born of a few tiny little white lies that have crept in recently.

You love to make a plan-of-attack
Scorpio, of course you do – who
wouldn't want to take action to ensure
their own success? But you are such
a calculating water sign, you must
beware not to overstrategize...
this is more a game of chance
than a game of chess.

Guard against the ego's desire to rule; feeding it at all costs is a mistake, as you run the risk of it taking over, and spreading poison and destruction. Aim for balance.

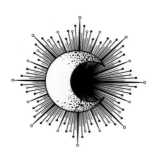

Adversity often brings
opportunity, and you are super-skilled
at pinpointing potential. See past the
immediate issue to what likely
lies ahead. You don't need to plan
every step along the way to
get there just yet.

Prioritize your loved ones and nurture your relationships, rather than allowing your attention to be distracted by what looks like an easy win. This one is not for you.

Over-thinking will not serve
you Scorpio. Do not devote too
much of your precious time to this.

Circumstances may not be quite as they seem and, as such, picking your way through this situation might take hard work. Resilience is required.

Allow your head to rule over your heart on this occasion Scorpio. Make your decision clean and logical.

Scorpio is a pleasure-loving
sign and this can take many forms
for you – spiritual, physical, emotional
and intellectual. Find the one that fits
best today and sink into it. You
need to recharge.

You are a sign of true light
and dark Scorpio – encourage the light
through your deep understanding
and empathy, and use your
high-functioning intuition to
balance the dark.

It is unusual for you to miss a single detail, although most often you keep the depth of this knowledge to yourself. Use your gifts wisely.

That deep-running vein of intuition, which touches everything you do, can be both a blessing and a curse. Resist the urge to act impulsively and hold back rather than striking too quickly. More will follow.

Stay active Scorpio – if all
that frustration and adrenaline
builds up it may sour and stagnate.
Keep movement at the forefront of
everything you do right now; let the
energy flow through.

You keep your truth close to your chest Scorpio and, with your feeling that there is always a game to be won or lost, who can blame you? But you shouldn't expect others to comprehend what is truly in your heart unless you tell them. Remember that not everyone is as intuitive as you are.

Take the easier route this time if you can, there are plenty of options. Keep a clear head and travel light.

Protect your reserves of strength carefully Scorpio; as a water sign, the tide can ebb and flow for you when it comes to energy. While you are quick to see that adversity often brings learning opportunities, you must pick your battles wisely.

Don't let it get under your skin if, just once in a while, you don't feel you receive *quite* the acknowledgement you deserve. Offer it up, then let it go.

It can seem a real struggle trying to cope with issues arising from changes imposed on you or those not of your choosing. Allow that sometimes this is just how it is and maintain a steadfast approach without engaging or actively opposing more than you have to.

Things in your life are rarely static; as the sign of destruction and restoration, your one constant is, ironically, that everything shifts. Hold this knowledge as a positive and allow yourself to flow around the rest. You are a water sign, after all. Be more water.

Hard work and focus will bring the success you want; simple as that.

Put some time into building and nurturing those relationships Scorpio; you can't expect that they will just be there waiting for you when you need them if you don't put in that essential maintenance along the way.

It is important to devote some serious energy to achieving a sustainable balance between the different parts of your life; each must support the others for harmony to resonate.

Commit to restoring perspective and dedicating quality time to what matters. It is all too easy for a Scorpio to get swept away in the flash fires and excitement of issues clamouring loudest for your attention; do not neglect the truly important (but often quieter) things.

You recognize a good idea when you hear one, no matter what previously negative experiences you might have had with the messenger. Your competitive nature will not stand in the way of adopting a solid and sustainable solution. Defend the idea and give credit where it is due.

To answer this one, it is important to pay attention to your dreams Scorpio, but do not mistake them for reality. Your subconscious is not a particularly literal communicator.

Even valuable insight can be
confusing out of context. It's important
to be absolutely clear about
what you know.

A little distance is required Scorpio. Mind your own business, pull back a little and find your own way. The right thing will land with you soon enough.

Your power-surge requires
an outlet Scorpio – listen to that
itch in your muscles and get moving.
Challenge yourself, feel the burn and
re-oxygenate the blood pumping
through your veins; you will feel
a million times better afterwards,
in every way.

Ups and downs are all part of life Scorpio... but if you don't feel you are getting what you need then it is time to take a closer look at what's going on. Do you feel you've missed an opportunity, or that something you nearly got off the ground stalled at the crucial moment? See what you can do to fire things up or reignite them.

Keep your powder dry
Scorpio, bide your time.

It will be vital to be honest
with yourself as well as others in
relation to this issue. Self-knowledge
is never a weakness and allowing
yourself to be seen is a
particular strength.

Your impulse is to stay the course and maintain that hard line until you get the results you are striving for. But there is nothing more to be gained with this one, holding on longer than anyone else will just drag you down.

Risk is necessary when you are aiming for those big rewards. But if you are asking yourself 'What have I got to lose?' too often, it might be a sign you should pull back a little.

Do you finally feel like you have found your comfort zone, or are you simply stuck in a rut? Only you can answer this one Scorpio. Once you do so truthfully, you will know what to do next.

Following your feelings rather than sticking to strategy at the moment will inject a much-needed jolt of direction and clarity into your life. There may even be changes you feel compelled to make – don't over-think things, just go with your heart.

Take a detour from your usual determined problem-solving style this time Scorpio; work around the immediate issue, modify your expectations and be willing to adopt a much more flexible approach.

Harbouring resentments is an unfortunate Scorpio trait, but part of the package. You're tough-minded and this flows through to your treatment of others as well as the criticism-loop you are inclined to play yourself. Ease up. You are not really as in control as you might think, so relaxing a little won't do any harm.

Allow others their voice rather
than waving that stinging tail around
casually, intimidating them into biting
their own tongues. It might take others
a little longer to get to the point than
it takes you but be patient. They
may very well have valuable
information to share.

Your choices have an inevitable knock-on for those around you, especially those who share this space or interest. Obviously, you can't control the outcome for everyone (and why would you want to?). But do consider likely repercussions before you wriggle into a hole you might not be easily able to escape from.

You're a thrill-seeker Scorpio, but your excitement-hunts can include an unnerving level of control as well. You definitely say 'yes' to the fun, but you want to be part of making it happen. Try a different way this time – go with the flow, just as an experiment, and see what happens.

The key to tackling this
slightly sticky issue will be
allowing rather than blocking.
Agree, go along with it and find
a way, rather than shutting it
down the first chance you get.

Pull back inside yourself when you feel the need to regroup and recalibrate; do not fight what your body, mind and soul are telling you they need right now.

Check in honestly with yourself to be sure you are not sacrificing too much. Is this taking a toll on your physical, emotional or mental health... or perhaps all three? If not, fantastic. If so, you will need to prioritize where to best spend your efforts.

Resolving this one will depend on locating the middle ground. It may not seem as appealing and exciting to a Scorpio as some of the other options, but the worst thing you could do right now would be to bite off more than you can chew.

Allowing others the time and space
to feel heard when they want to
engage with you can test your Scorpio
(im)patience, but, really, they are not
asking that much of you. Sometimes
just your presence is enough.

Context is all when it comes to making comparisons; almost anything can be made to look good by comparing it with something worse. Try to judge this situation on its own merits.

If you are blessed with extra energy right now Scorpio, make good use of it to get plenty done. Further down the road, you'll be pleased you did.

Potential paths will spring up on all sides as you adopt a warm and encouraging attitude to others around you. If they are trying to turn to you as a leader, don't fight it Scorpio. You have the perfect blend of skills to do a brilliant job.

It is vital that you stay active
Scorpio. Clearing anything that
doesn't serve you and maintaining
energy flow in the right direction, will
keep all on track for a positive result.

Often mistaken for a fire sign because of your more explosive traits, your power is actually drawn from emotion. Because of this, you can easily become spiritually drained if you don't take the time to replenish your reserves. Nurture yourself.

Even when you want to be alone
Scorpio, you still have a need to feel
that you belong. Respect your need
for separation but bear the group in
mind; community and connection are
vital for your survival.

Say what you need to say
now Scorpio; holding back any
longer may mean you miss your
opportunity. Peace will only be
restored if you are able to open up
and talk this one through. You will
need to be bold and honest.

Pushing the limits is not usually a problem for you Scorpio – you are never one to simply stagnate in your comfort zone. Set any indecision or fear aside and push yourself. You are capable of much more than you thought once you make a conscious decision to challenge the logic behind self-set constraints.

Acquisitions and material wealth
have no intrinsic value on their own;
enriching your family and community
will create positive ripples that
reach a long, long way.

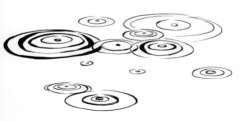

Wield that powerful sting carefully Scorpio; your anger, or frustration, can spark a dangerous storm. Take this one step at a time and be mindful of your own strength and forcefulness. Keep your temper in check lest you accidentally poison someone you weren't even aiming for.

Your deeply strategic (some might even say cunning) style means that rarely, if ever, does anything escape you Scorpio. Staying on high-alert all the time can exhaust your reserves though – it's important to allow yourself a break from the adrenaline occasionally.

Adding a bit more fun into your daily schedule is sure to reap rewards Scorpio; there's more than one way to play this game and introducing some flexibility will be beneficial in more ways than one.

When you're not sure which way to turn, don't forget that you can lean on those around you until you feel ready to pick yourself up and carry on again. For someone as self-sufficient as you, this may feel strange. But it will be a positive move for all concerned, resulting in stronger connections and deepened trust.

Tackling this one might be easier if you appeal to the logic rather than the feelings of others. Spend your time working with the facts, rather than discussing emotions, and they will be more likely to support your position.

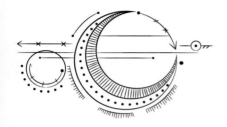

Ask for what you need,
loudly and clearly, without leaving
any room for potential confusion or
misunderstanding. Say it as it is,
then reap the rewards.

Reaching a compromise isn't
usually the way you roll Scorpio, but
it might be the best thing to do on this
occasion. Give a little, take a little,
then you can all move on.

Finding a way to scuttle around this problem, rather than wasting energy attacking it head-on, will put you in a much better position to deepen your understanding (and it might just elevate your moral high-ground position as well).

Learning methods for venting
your frustrations without negatively
impacting others will likely be life-long
work for you Scorpio. Your trademark
venomous sting is typically delivered
without warning. You may feel better
for the release, but your victims
invariably come away feeling
a whole lot worse.

That sharp connection, that perfect 'click' of recognition and acknowledgement – there's nothing quite like it Scorpio. But before you can find your people, you need to let them see you. Time to step out from the shadows for a little while and show up as yourself.

Keep your impulse to control under, er, control Scorpio. There is so much you cannot influence... Work on the bits you can work on, leave the rest and trust in fate. What is yours will come to you.

Persistent and strategic, you can be coolly calculating when it comes to getting what you want Scorpio. Don't forget to include some contingency for the inevitable time-cost if other people are also involved. Perhaps making some allowances for a little warmth and human connection could be a good idea as well...

You are courageous and curious Scorpio, fascinated by a mystery and endlessly drawn to the hidden and seemingly unsolvable. Combined with that little 'control' thing you've got going on, this all makes you a bit of a super-sleuth. Playing detective might help you uncover a few hidden gems; keep them up your sleeve for later.

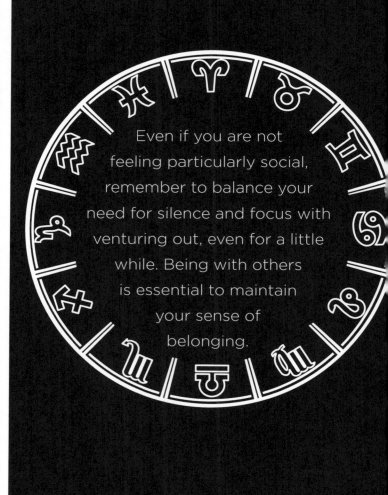

Even if you are not feeling particularly social, remember to balance your need for silence and focus with venturing out, even for a little while. Being with others is essential to maintain your sense of belonging.

The ability to focus and concentrate comes naturally to single-minded Scorpios. Remember to temper these talents with your broader gifts for empathy and understanding, to keep everything toned and functioning like a well-oiled machine. None of your facets exists in isolation.

It is vital that you maintain a straightforward and honest approach to those around you, as well as yourself. Your heart may be guiding you towards choosing an easy way around, so be sure you balance this with some crystal-clear reasoning.

You know precisely what you want and you are willing to put in the time and effort to figure out how to get it. If that makes you 'cunning' and 'calculating', so be it. Most people would just call it smart.

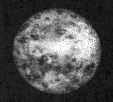

Mars, as your co-ruling planet, brings both temper and courage. It also means you have reserves of passionate determination to draw on should your outward energy need a boost. Draw on this secret store when you need it most.

Scorpio is a fixed sign, so your tendency is more towards absorbing than transmitting; with water as your element, you are strongly interconnected and a tuned-in sensitivity flows through everything you do. Pay attention to your intuition and the messages it is feeding through to your conscious, thinking mind.

Insisting on loyalty from those close to you is simply good sense Scorpio. If you suspect someone is not being straight, or that they are adopting underhand techniques to sneak into first place, take a big step back. You don't want to be caught up in the inevitable fallout.

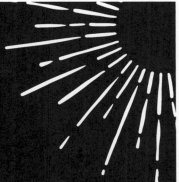

That famous Scorpion intuition
and tenacity, coupled with your
ambition and your love of reward,
make you an unstoppable force once
your heart is set on a goal. Draw on
these gifts now and use them wisely.

Assuming someone has crossed you is often your first go-to, but it activates a knee-jerk rather than a carefully considered response. Has the same thing happened again? Weigh up all possibilities, ask some questions and then apply some cold, clean logic to work this one out.

Feedback is not always required;
it's time to bite your tongue. Mindful
listening is a rare and valuable skill,
and you will only get the hang
of it with practice.

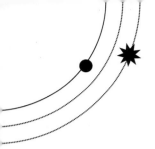

Just like your quick-stinging constellation creature, you do have something of a reputation for inflicting sudden and surprising damage if cornered. Open your eyes and your mind to the positives that revising your position and reconsidering your response might bring your way.

Ambition and dedication are second nature to you – laziness is definitely not a Scorpio trait. But it is time to assess whether the effort versus reward equation is as balanced as you would like it to be. Working doggedly to no end makes no sense.

Your silence is often assumed to be secrecy Scorpio... and sometimes it is. But when it comes to others keeping secrets from you, your immediate suspicion is aroused. Allow others the benefit of the doubt though; they may have very good reasons for keeping things close to their chests.

Although you typically operate
in quite an insular fashion Scorpio,
you should feel pleased and proud
when those close to you succeed.
It is likely that you have been
the role-model they needed, and
your strength and long-game
technique is an inspiration.

Teasing out some space between your personal life and your work is a crucial survival technique Scorpio, especially for someone so dedicated. You will not be the only one to benefit from the resulting perspective and room to breathe.

Emotional knots can take a long time to untangle Scorpio, and first you must be certain you are ready to tackle this one. Are you sure you're not still holding on to it as part of your 'story'? Take it slowly and ask for help if you need it. There is no prescribed finish line for this work.

Intuition can be both a blessing
and a curse, and for you an intrinsic
part of pretty much every move
you make. It can lead you to act
impulsively; you must be careful not
to turn too quickly with this one.

Take your foot off the accelerator Scorpio. There is no point making a start until you have a proper plan in place.

You are used to being the one in charge Scorpio, so it can feel extremely frustrating when someone else's behaviour hurts or confuses you. If you allow this to continue, it will impact your own confidence and effectiveness. Take control and get to the root of the problem quickly.

You don't like being kept in the dark Scorpio. Not one bit. You need to find out what's going on and if you need to ambush someone into revealing the truth, then so be it.

Negative news or abrasive feedback might feel unwarranted and may provoke your strong defence response. Before that deadly sting of yours takes aim, pause to consider whether this criticism might be less about you and more about them. Arguing your point may simply not be worth it this time. Rise above it.

Scorpios are so self-sufficient that operating as part of a team can sometimes not feel worth it. If you have to work in a group, and you're feeling insular, keep yourself to yourself as much as you can.

Deeply intense relationships
are just the way it goes for you
Scorpio; whether with friends, family,
colleagues or lovers, you want more.
Know this about yourself and make an
effort to keep it light right now – some
people might be wary of getting too
close too quickly, but they may
be worth waiting for.

Tread cautiously Scorpio; things
might not be quite as they first look.
Don't administer that fatal sting; you
may realize too late that you made
a mistake. Easy does it.

Reinforcing shared values with friends or a partner is important at the moment Scorpio. Pick an activity that makes you all feel you are making a positive difference and get stuck in.

Take care that your famous Scorpio ambition doesn't tip over into a darker and hungrier desire for control. Reassure yourself: you are all that you need to be. You are already enough.

With water as your ruling element,
it's no surprise that your dark intensity
can sometimes seem to reach
unfathomable depths. Relax your grip
a little and relinquish your instinct
to withhold... there is beauty in
darkness as well as light.

You thought you were
watching closely Scorpio, but perhaps
something slipped past you...
Expect the unexpected.

A surprising turn of events might flip your radar into overdrive. If you suspect trickery, reverse out of the situation as quickly as you can. If it's just something you hadn't foreseen, learn and move on.

If you find yourself charging into obstacles every way you turn, perhaps it's time to stay still for a while Scorpio. Let the flux settle, then try again.

Too many setbacks can
rapidly drain momentum and,
more importantly, they can knock
your confidence. If you find yourself in
the middle of a sticky patch and it is
difficult to keep moving, perhaps
use this time differently Scorpio.
Reassess and plan afresh.

When the urge to take action
is upon you Scorpio, you are
unstoppable. If now is one of those
times, make the most of it and whirl
through that list that has been backing
up in your head. You never know
quite how long these super-charged
go-faster stages might last...

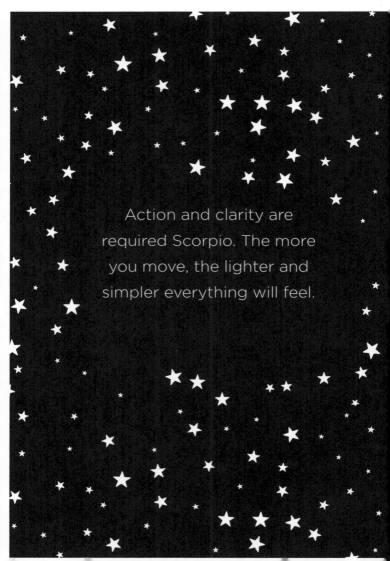

Action and clarity are required Scorpio. The more you move, the lighter and simpler everything will feel.

Take advantage of opportunities
to work remotely or stay in and enjoy
some seclusion if you can Scorpio.
Your charging energy, and the threat
of that hovering tail-stinger, might
otherwise prove less than conducive
to getting things done.

When a supercharge of energy strikes, be sure you are able to make best use of it Scorpio. As long as everything else is taken care of, you will be able to sail with the prevailing winds to achieve excellent results.

Brave, loyal, trustworthy and
honest, you are a gift of a friend
Scorpio, and having you onside is a
monumental plus for all who love you.
Even if you are excited by new, fresh
opportunities, don't forget to include
those who have stood by you
all this time.

Determination is a defining
Scorpio characteristic, and one
that can sometimes tip over into
bloody-mindedness if you are not
careful to keep your ego and ambition
in check. Ambition is admirable.
Ruthlessness, less so.

Openness and humility are
required right now; allowing yourself
to be receptive and vulnerable will
mean you have a much stronger
chance of learning what you
need to know.

Aim as high and as far as the furthest stars you can see Scorpio; this is a time to channel all that amazing creativity into some big dreams and lofty ambitions. Then you will really see what you are capable of.

Your only limitation will be your own self-belief Scorpio. That's not to say you should be deliberately unrealistic, but, for now, you should focus more on the 'what' and less on the 'how'. There will be plenty of time for practicalities further down the road.

It may feel as though you are struggling to keep order Scorpio, but perhaps instead of fighting to assert control you should consider this from another angle... Is there something you have overlooked that the universe is trying to reveal to you? Is there a pattern or a missing piece of the puzzle just out of sight?

Staying connected and in communication will help you ride this one out Scorpio. The temptation, of course, is to draw inwards and wait for it to all blow over. But if you shelter too far inside, you might still be in hiding long after the storm has passed.

Fun holds an important role
in keeping things fresh, helping
you engage with the present and,
ultimately, in affirming that you are in
the right place and it's all been worth
it. So, let that silly Scorpion inside
out to play for a while; it will
do you good.

A focus on home is important
right now Scorpio; perhaps for you
that means decluttering, a renovation
project, moving to a new house or
making more time for home-based
hobbies or work. Make your home
into the place where you want
to be and come back to.

Keep your mind clear and your eyes open right now Scorpio. There is plenty going on that you need to be aware of. Be open, awake and receptive, and note the details.

All intuitive signs have strong reactions to the energy of other people, but when you really take against someone it's useful to have a reason Scorpio. Best to keep it to yourself for now; watch and wait, but be wary.

Difficult or odd behaviour in others often has an intriguing explanation... take some time to find out more about someone who might seem a little awkward in the days ahead.

There will always be people you don't like, and maybe even people you do like who don't like you (unimaginable as that might seem). The impulse to control and convince is strong with you Scorpio, but ultimately it is freeing yourself from concern about others and their opinions that will give you the greatest strength.

There is a beauty in the basic, practical, day-to-day tasks that keep your body nourished, your household running smoothly and your living space clean and calm. Leave more intellectual pursuits for another time, and revel in this opportunity for some beautiful mindfulness.

Highly emotional, loyal, passionate and great fun – what's not to like in a Scorpio? Well, the intensity can get a little heavy sometimes, and others might find the suspicion and need for control tricky to handle occasionally as well... Keep it light for a while if you can, save that other stuff for another time.

Avoidance isn't the best technique for you Scorpio, it never seems to pay off in the way you hope it will. Processing your feelings during difficult times, although painful, is infinitely better than shoving them all down into an emotional powder keg and hoping the lid will stay on... Invariably, it does not.

Others seek you out because
your warmth and zingy intuition
means you connect quickly and
closely. You 'get' people. They like that.
Be sure not to misuse this particular
Scorpio skill of yours. If they think you
are becoming close friends and then
confide in you, but you simply see
information and potential, there
will be repercussions.

It's not that you're materialistic, necessarily, it's just that there are a lot of things you want. You know, really, that none of them will bring true happiness. Family, friends and your own spiritual and emotional wellbeing are where you should invest to see true value materialize.

While the dark side visits you
more often than it shows up for other
signs, luck is also on your team more
frequently than perhaps you realize.
Time to broaden your personal
definition of wealth out a bit. For a
dark-side lover with a venomous sting,
things actually seem to be going
pretty well, right?

When the impulse to get things done strikes Scorpio, be sure you grab it with both hands. Powering through that to-do list will bring multiple benefits right now, not least a freshened-up living space, a tidier mind and clear decks ready for what comes next.

Check in honestly with yourself to be sure you are not sacrificing too much right now Scorpio – that relentless dedication of yours will eat up every scrap of your energy if you allow it to. You will need to prioritize where to best spend your efforts.

Quick temper and anger can be signs of sadness and stress. The urge to push others away when one is hurting or confused is not solely a Scorpio trait, but your particular power means that perhaps you do it more forcefully than others. Try a different way, allow yourself to be vulnerable and confide in others.

Leaning on the people around you for love and support is perfectly allowable Scorpio. They may be pleasantly surprised, even flattered, by your level of trust in them and your willingness to share.

Devoting a little more time and focus to the goals you want to achieve will certainly reap rewards Scorpio. Re-establish your targets and re-affirm your commitment to reaching them.

Appealing to others' logic and intellect, rather than their emotions, is the best way to go right now Scorpio. Spend time explaining the facts, rather than messing around with feelings, and you will find they are better able to understand (and perhaps even support) your position.

Staying connected and content might be simpler than you think. Busy your hands with practical tasks and your body with satisfying, repetitive work. Leave thinking and planning for another day, and instead notice the movement of light and dark through the day and night. Be content with what you have and don't ask for more than you need.

Giving in and reaching a compromise are two different things Scorpio, and, let's be honest, neither really appeals to you. But if middle ground must be found then give it some clean, focused thought and decide how far you are willing to go before entering negotiations.

Keep your sting tucked away Scorpio. This problem is one to gently feel your way around rather than clash with head on. Deepening your understanding may give you a new vantage point, which could help you see fresh opportunities heading your way.

It won't take others by surprise
if you ask for what you want. But
including a little generosity and
understanding in your request will
make the world of difference.
Resources are not unlimited, so be
mindful of the needs of others.

The flow of your feelings is close under your skin at the best of times Scorpio; right now you should pay particular attention to the direction you feel compelled to follow. There may be changes you should make.

With the use of your intuition and strong problem-solving skills, and with the addition of just a pinch of logic and diplomacy, you should have this one sorted to everyone's satisfaction in no time at all.

Pay attention to what you are feeling Scorpio. But, at the same time, understand that it might not be all about what is currently going on; your subconscious has a way of jumping out from dark places to surprise you every so often, to remind you of the issues you still need to deal with.

Stubborn Scorpio? You?
The interpretation depends on the
one making the judgement; do not
concern yourself with the opinions of
others when you know you are
on the right track.

This doesn't have to be an either/or situation Scorpio. Find a way to indulge in your imaginative side, just ensure all the practicalities are taken care of first.

Do not waste any more
time on this.

If your hyper-keen intuition is picking up negativity and shady energy from another source, whatever form it takes, preserve your own boundaries and build in a little distance. Do not allow the backward-facing stance of others to stunt your growth or limit your own progress.

When it comes to honesty
and loyalty, be sure you are giving as
good as you insist on getting.

First published in Great Britain in 2021 by
Greenfinch
An imprint of Quercus Editions Ltd
Carmelite House
50 Victoria Embankment
London EC4Y 0DZ

An Hachette UK company

A CIP catalogue record for this book is available
from the British Library.

HB ISBN 978-1-52941-228-4

10 9 8 7 6 5 4 3 2 1

Designed by Ginny Zeal
Cover design by Andrew Smith
Text by Susan Kelly
All images from Shutterstock.com

Printed and bound in China.

Papers used by Greenfinch are from well-managed forests
and other responsible sources.